Tell Me
About
Faith

Published in Nashville, Tennessee, by Tommy Nelson®, a Division of Thomas Nelson, Inc.

Tommy Nelson® books may be purchased in bulk for educational, business, fund-raising, or sales promotional use. For information, please email SpecialMarkets@ThomasNelson.com.

Scripture quotations in this book are from the *International Children's Bible*®, *New Century Version*®, © 1986, 1988, 1999 by Tommy Nelson®, a Division of Thomas Nelson, Inc. All rights reserved.

Library of Congress Cataloging-in-Publication Data

Anderson, Joel.
  Tell me about faith / by Joel Anderson ; illustrated by Joel Anderson and Kristi Carter Smith.
      p. cm. — (Big topics for little kids)
  ISBN 1-4003-0615-9 (hardcover)
1. Faith—Juvenile literature. I. Smith, Kristi Carter. II. Title.
  BV4637.A62 2005
  234'.23—dc22

                                        2005000011

Printed in China

05 06 07 08 09 RRD 5 4 3 2 1

Tell Me About Faith

by Joel Anderson

*Illustrated by Joel Anderson
and Kristi Carter Smith*

Tommy NELSON®

www.tommynelson.com

A Division of Thomas Nelson, Inc.
www.ThomasNelson.com

*Faith means being sure
of the things we hope for.
And faith means knowing
that something is real
even if we do not see it.*

HEBREWS 11:1

It was a hopeful time for three people.

Two were at home.

And one was far away.

The two at home talked about the one they loved.
They knew he loved them, too,
even though they couldn't see him.

The one who was far away thought about home.
He knew his wife and daughter were praying for him,
even though he couldn't hear them.

He remembered the day he went to war.
His little girl was just a baby then.

She couldn't remember being with her daddy,
but the little girl thought about him often.

Someday, she would hold his hand and walk
with him in the garden he had planted.

Even though the little girl couldn't hug her daddy,
she could feel his love in the letters he wrote.

His letters made her feel safe, they told her she was precious, and they promised he would be home again.

The little girl did her best
to let her daddy know
she loved him.

He did his best to make sure
his wife and daughter had
everything they needed.

Months went by, and one summer day
a package arrived.

Inside were three ugly brown things
and one pretty card.

For my girls,

These bulbs aren't pretty now...
but plant them
in the garden this fall.
Wait all winter,
and when spring comes,
I will be home
to enjoy the pretty
flowers with you!

I miss you SO much!
Love,
Daddy

When fall came, the little girl dug three holes in the garden,
dropped in the bulbs, and covered them with dirt.
Then she and her mommy waited.

Weeks and months went by.
And nothing happened.

But the little girl never stopped believing
that springtime would come . . .

. . . the snow would melt,

the flowers would bloom,

and she would finally see her daddy.

And that is exactly what happened.

We always have courage.
We know that while we
live in this body,
we are away from the Lord.
We live by what we believe,
not by what we can see.

2 CORINTHIANS 5:6–7

Parent / Teacher Discussion Aid

Q. What is faith?
A. It is believing in something you can't see; knowing something to be true, even though you can't prove it. Faith is putting your trust in someone else besides yourself. It is trusting in a promise, hoping, waiting, and looking for what you know is sure to happen.

Q. In whom or what do you trust?
A. You trust that a chair will hold you up and not crash to the ground each time you sit down. You trust the lights to turn on each time you flick on a light switch. You trust your parents to feed you each time you are hungry. You trust in God to hear you each time you pray.

Q. How did the little girl in this story show her faith?
A. She believed she had a daddy who loved her, even though she could not remember meeting him. She never stopped believing, hoping, and trusting in his promise that one day he would come home and she would see him face-to-face.

Q. How can you show your faith?
A. Obedience is faith. When you do what the Bible says is right, you are proving that you have faith in God's rules. God's rules help us to know Him. When we obey His commands, we show the whole world that we have faith in God. When you obey your parents, you are showing them that you love them and you believe they know what is best for you. Another way to show your faith is to pray. Even though you can't see God, He is right here with you. He can see you and hear you. When you talk to Him, you show your faith by believing He is right here. When God answers your prayers, you can show your faith by thanking Him for His goodness.

Q. Can God give me more faith?

A. Yes! Jesus talked about sending a Helper to show us how to have more faith. This Helper is called the Holy Spirit, or the Spirit of Truth. He teaches our heart how to know right from wrong, gives us faith to believe in God, and helps us to obey God's rules.

Jesus said that if we love Him, we will obey His commands. He will ask the Father to give us another Helper to be with us forever. The Helper is the Spirit of Truth. The world cannot accept Him, because it does not see Him or know Him. But we know Him, because He lives with us and He will be in us (John 14:15–17).

Experiment for Little People

TOOLS
Blindfold (optional)

Close your eyes (or use a blindfold) and try to walk across the room. It's difficult, isn't it?

Now do it again. But have someone hold your hand and lead you across the room. It's easier, isn't it? Why? Because you put your trust in someone who can see.

That is how it is with God. He sees everything. He knows everything. His rules are to help us live life without stumbling. It takes faith to do what is right. It takes trust to follow His ways.